100 Ques
and Answers
About Arab
Americans

Michigan State University
School of Journalism

Read The Spirit Books

an imprint of
David Crumm Media, LLC
Canton, Michigan

For more information and further discussion, visit
news.jrn.msu.edu/culturalcompetence/

Cover art and design by
Rick Nease
www.RickNeaseArt.com

Published By
Read The Spirit Books
an imprint of
David Crumm Media, LLC
42015 Ford Rd., Suite 234
Canton, Michigan, USA

For information about customized editions, bulk purchases
or permissions, contact David Crumm Media, LLC at info@
DavidCrummMedia.com

Contents

Acknowledgments

This guide is part of a series in cultural competence published by the Michigan State University School of Journalism. It is descended from a guide for journalists funded in 2000 by Knight Ridder, Inc., and created by people at the Detroit Free Press and others. Knight Ridder support for the original project came from Jacqui Love Marshall and Reginald A. Stuart. Two people who worked on that project and helped create this revision are David Crumm and Joe Grimm.

This guide has been updated, refocused and re-organized. It was then reviewed by:

- Jack G. Shaheen, a distinguished visiting professor at New York University
- Rana Elmir, deputy director, American Civil Liberties Union, Michigan
- Osama Siblani, editor and publisher of The Arab American News
- Suzanne Manneh, New America Media
- Matthew Jaber Stiffler and Jaber Saad of the Arab American National Museum in Dearborn

- Abed Hammoud, assistant U.S. attorney at United States Attorney's Office, Detroit
- Raphael Calis, international journalist and former executive editor and vice president at United Press International
- Haifa Fakhouri, president and CEO, Arab American and Chaldean Council
- Jeffrey Ghannam, managing director, Democratech Solutions, LLC

This guide is published by Read the Spirit Books and the Michigan State University School of Journalism.

If you have suggestions for this guide, would like to know more about the series or order in quantity, we'd love to hear from you.

Joe Grimm, series editor
joe.grimm@gmail.com

Foreword

"Too often we hold fast to the clichés of our forebears."

– President John F. Kennedy

This guide provides accurate information to readers, enabling them to make informed decisions about Americans with Arab roots that are based on facts, not mythologies.

We should never underestimate the power of mythology, cautioned President Kennedy. "Myths are legion and the truth hard to find," he wrote, adding that the "great enemy of the truth is very often not the lie—deliberate, contrived, and dishonest—but the myth—persistent, persuasive and unrealistic."

History teaches us that entrenched myths and/or stereotypes about a people—via the Internet and/or mainstream media outlets—do our country a disservice. All too often, stereotypes result in barriers that translate into false reporting, which is greater today than ever before.

Unlike some of America's racial and ethnic groups, Arab Americans were invisible for decades in American media—they had no identity. Subsequently, the vast majority were not subjected to damaging stereotypes—until the tragedy of 9/11 dramatically altered perceptions. Abruptly, journalists and imagemakers wrapped themselves into straitjackets of stereotypes.

Dozens of American television shows, ranging from 24 to Sleeper Cell, introduced a new threatening stereotype, the Arab American Neighbor as Terrorist. These programs drilled this mythology into our living rooms. News reports and screen images implied that regardless of our roots, faith or skin color, we ran shadowy sleeper cells inside warehouses and mosques, from Los Angeles to Washington, D.C. Few, if any, distinctions were made between Arabs and Americans, between Muslims and Muslim Americans. All the bad guys blended together. The seen one, seen 'em all cliché pummeled home the mythology. Is it any wonder some of us viewed American citizens with Arab roots as a threat?

Fortunately, generalizations about an Arab American public, a people who hail from 22 different Arab countries, will eventually cease. We have come a long way since the dark days after 9/11 when fear, ignorance and stereotypes ran rampant. This indispensable, much-needed guide will help us move forward and debunk mythologies. We are more likely to embrace the wisdom of Hillary Clinton who reminds us, "The vast majority of Arabs and Muslims in the United States are loyal citizens. (Their) daily lives revolve around work, family and community … It's not fair to apply a negative stereotype to all (Arabs) and Muslims."

Not fair indeed.

Jack G. Shaheen

Kennedy's commencement address at Yale University, June 11, 1962.

Clinton's remarks were made during a 1986 White House Prayer breakfast.

About this Guide

Like all people, Arab Americans are too often described in generalities. Although the Arab culture is one of the oldest on Earth, it is misunderstood in many parts of the United States. There are no easy, one-size-fits-all answers for any group of people. Culture, language and religion are distinct qualities that combine in different ways to connect Arabs to each other and to non-Arabs, as well as to distinguish some Arabs from others. In a word, it's complicated. That is the first lesson. There are at least 100 more things to learn in this guide to cultural competence.

The differences that seem to separate Arab Americans from non-Arabs can be much smaller than the variations that differentiate them from one another. It takes time to learn the issues and to understand them, but it is essential and rewarding to do that. Misunderstanding ultimately hurts each one of us.

The 100 questions and answers you have here only touch briefly on the issues. But we urge you to start with these, continue to read, talk with people and make a long-term commitment to understanding. True understanding does not come with a hundred questions, or even a thousand, but each question helps.

About the Series

This series of guides to cultural competence is designed to use journalistic tools to replace bias and stereotypes with information. Guides are published by the Michigan State University School of Journalism. We create guides that are factual, clear and accessible.

This guide has its roots in the 1990s, when the first edition of this guide was published. It became the model for this series.

Today, the series uses interviews and keyword analysis to determine questions. It follows a four-dimensional editing ethic of respect, accuracy, authority and accessibility.

Guides are intended to be the first step to more conversations and greater understanding.

Overview

1 Who are Arab Americans?

Arab Americans are U.S. citizens or permanent residents who trace their ancestry to, or who immigrated from, Arabic-speaking places in the Middle East. That is in southwestern Asia and northern Africa. Not all people in this region are Arabs. Most Arab Americans were born in the United States.

2 How many Arab Americans are there?

This is unclear. A May 2013 report by the U.S. Census Bureau's American Community Survey said that the number of people saying they had Arab ancestry grew 76 percent from 850,000 in 1990 to an estimated 1.5 million in 2006-2010. However, the Arab American Institute, based on its own research, estimates that this population is closer to 5 million.

3 In which states do Arab Americans live?

Arab Americans live in all 50 states. According to the U.S. Census Bureau's American Community Survey data for 2005-2009, about a third are in California (272,485), Michigan (191,607) and New York (149,729). Another third are in these seven states: Illinois, Maryland, Massachusetts,

New Jersey, Ohio, Texas and Virginia. The Arab American Institute said there is significant under reporting that might mean the actual population is 817,455 in California and 500,000 in Michigan.

4 How are they distributed by nationality?

According to the Arab American Institute, Lebanese Americans, the largest group of Arab Americans, are also the largest group in most states. Exceptions include Georgia, New Jersey and Tennessee, which have larger numbers of people of Egyptian descent. In Arizona, the institute says, people of Moroccan descent are the largest group, while Rhode Island has more people of Syrian descent. People of Sudanese descent lead in Nebraska and South Dakota. People of Palestinian descent, who are most numerous in California, have their greatest concentration in Illinois.

5 What are the population centers for Arab Americans?

The institute estimates that 94 percent of Arab Americans live in metropolitan areas. The top five are Los Angeles, Detroit, New York/New Jersey, Chicago and Washington, D.C.

6 Do Arab Americans come from a shared language tradition?

For Arab people globally, the Arabic language is one of the great unifying and distinguishing characteristics. This is generally referred to as Classical Arabic. Even so, colloquial Arabic differs so much that people of different dialects can have trouble conversing. There are several categories: Levantine dialect (Jordan, Syria, Palestine, Lebanon), Egyptian and North African dialect, and Khalijji, or Gulf, dialect. Modern Standard Arabic (Classical Arabic) is a pan-Arabic language used in formal letters, books and print and broadcast media. It is also spoken at Middle East peace conferences and on television news. Quranic (or Koranic) Arabic is also a widely spoken form of the language, but it differs from Modern Standard Arabic. Not all Arab Americans know Arabic. Many are second-, third- and fourth-generation Americans.

7 Do Arab Americans have a shared religion?

No. Arab Americans practice many religions, including Christianity, Islam, Druze, Judaism and others. Most Arab countries are predominantly Muslim. So are some non-Arab countries, such as Turkey and Indonesia. Although Arabs are connected by culture, they have different faiths. Culture and religion vary. While most Arabs in the world are Muslim, most Arabs in the United States are Christian.

8 What is the Middle East conflict all about?

A guide like this cannot adequately answer this question. The oldest conflicts in the Middle East are the Arab-Israeli conflict, the struggle over Palestine and independence movements. In addition to some serious differences between Arab countries and Israel, there are disagreements among and within Arab countries. The roots of these conflicts revolve around some of the world's oldest religions, ethnic differences, and boundaries drawn during

20th century European colonialism. More recently, Arab countries have experienced civil uprisings and revolutions that have led to regime changes. In the case of Tunisia, where the so-called Arab Spring began, a new constitution was adopted. In other Arab countries, political uprisings have remained unsettled and led to a civil war, such as in Syria. For more detailed answers, there are resources listed at the end of this guide.

9 How does conflict in the Middle East affect Arab Americans?

Because Arabs maintain close family ties, even when separated, and because Arab-American communities can include recent immigrants, many people have a keen, personal interest in news from the Middle East. When American interests are affected, the Arab American community can feel unfair scrutiny or physical and personal repercussions. A prime example of this occurred after the 9/11 attacks.

Origins

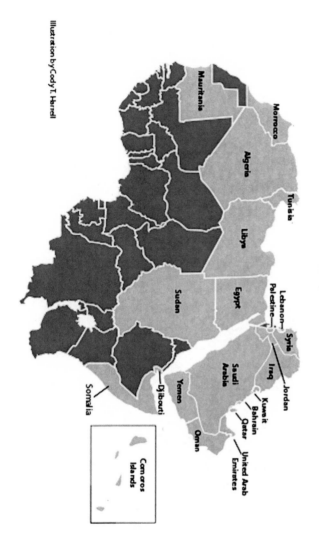

The Arab League

Illustration by Cody T. Harrell

10 What constitutes the Arab world?

The umbrella organization, the Arab League, has 22 members. They are Algeria, Bahrain, Comoros Islands, Djibouti, Egypt, Iraq, Jordan, Kuwait, Lebanon, Libya, Mauritania, Morocco, Oman, Palestine, Qatar, Saudi Arabia, Somalia, Sudan, Syria, Tunisia, United Arab Emirates and Yemen.

11 What is the breakdown in the United States?

These estimates are from the U.S. Census Bureau's American Community Survey for 2006-2010:

- Lebanese: 485,917
- Egyptian: 179,853
- Syrian: 147,426
- Palestinian: 83,241
- Moroccan: 74,908
- Iraqi: 73,896
- Jordanian: 60,056
- Yemeni: 29,358

12 Is Palestine a country?

Historically, Palestine was a country east of the Mediterranean Sea. Today the region includes current-day Israel. As a distinct region, Palestine was under Ottoman control (a Turkish empire) and then British control until 1948, when the nation of Israel was created. Areas of Palestine became Israel and part of Jordan. Today, Palestine refers to the territories under Palestine National Authority control in the West Bank, which remains under Israeli occupation and in the case of the Gaza Strip, contains a variety of Israeli strictures. The United Nations General Assembly in 2012 upgraded Palestine to a non-voting observer state. Palestinians share a collective national identity and are moving toward independence and self-rule as a country. Negotiations continue between Palestinian authorities and the Israeli government to find a permanent agreement. The Palestinian National Council is the parliament.

13 Isn't Iran an Arab country?

No. Although Iran borders Iraq, it originated in the Persian Empire and has a different language and cultural history from Arab countries. The dominant language in Iran is Farsi, not Arabic, although other languages are spoken there as well. Persian is sometimes used to describe either the language or the ethnicity, but Farsi and Iranian are not interchangeable. Iran's location, the fact that it is an Islamic country, and the similarity of its name to Iraq can confuse people.

14 So, not all people from the Middle East are Arabs?

That is correct. The four main language groups in the Middle East are Arabic, Hebrew, Persian and Turkish. Other significant language groups are Kurdish and Berber. Arabs are the biggest group in terms of population and land holdings, and this handbook focuses on people who have emigrated from or who are descended from people in those areas.

15 Are there other cultural groups from the Arab region?

Yes. Assyrians, Berbers, Chaldeans and Kurds have languages rooted in pre-Arab times. There also are religious differences. Chaldeans are the largest of these groups in the United States.

16 Who are Chaldeans?

Chaldeans are Catholics from Iraq. A religious and ethnic minority there, Chaldeans have some large communities in the United States, the largest in the Detroit and San Diego areas. The Chaldean Catholic Church has had connections with the Roman Catholic Church since 1551, and has been affiliated since 1830. The Chaldean Diocese of the Catholic Church in the United States has parishes in Michigan, California, Illinois and Arizona. It also has several missions. Churches offer Chaldean language services. Chaldeans and Assyrians, along with Arabs, are Semite people. The cultural foundation is similar, but the religious affiliation is different.

17 Are Chaldeans Arabs, or not?

Chaldeans and Arabs have cultural and political similarities, but different identities. The Chaldean language is different from Arabic. In Iraq, where Chaldeans originate, they are religiously distinct from the Muslim majority. While Chaldeans foster a separate identity, they also share an Iraqi nationality and share some concerns with Arabs. These nuances are lost by federal classifications, which sometimes reclassify Chaldeans as Arab or Iraqi. It is best to ask people how they identify themselves.

Language

18 Is Arabic the only language spoken within the Arab world?

No. For example, Assyrian and Chaldean services use a dialect of the original Aramaic. Other non-Arabic languages of the Middle East include Berber and Kurdish.

19 Do all Arab Americans speak one of these languages?

No. Remember that many Arab-American families have been in the United States for generations. Many, especially the younger generation, speak only English. Recent immigrants, since the middle of the 19th century and onward, would probably speak and use the Arabic language. But we don't assume that Arab Americans know the language of their ancestors, any more than we would assume that about other Americans.

20 Many recently immigrated Arab Americans also know French. Why is that?

Part of Arab history includes colonization by the French and British. In colonized countries, people in business and government had to know one or more European languages.

People who emigrated from countries that were once French colonies or mandates, including Lebanon, Tunisia, Morocco and Algeria, might be fluent in French.

21 Do schools in the Arab world teach other languages?

Definitely. That is one reason why it is much more common for Arab Americans to speak more than one language than it is for non-Arab Americans. Many immigrants come to the United States having learned two or three languages in their country of origin. Arab countries, like many others, emphasize the importance of knowing languages.

22 Is there any advice on pronouncing Arabic names?

Not really. It can be quite difficult to transliterate Arabic words into English. The languages have different sounds and English has fewer letters. Unless you know the Arabic alphabet, it's hard to know how to pronounce words correctly. The "r" sound is rolled, and there are characters for three different pronunciations of the "th" sound. Other sounds, such as the "gh" in Arabic, are difficult for speakers of English. Some Arabs who are new to English may find difficulty in pronouncing the "p" sound in English. For these reasons, English spellings of Arab words and names vary.

23 Is there any trick to spelling Arabic words?

There are so many variations that it is crucial to ask. Because Arabic and English characters and sounds are different, there is more than one way to transliterate the words. This is why the generally accepted English spelling of Mohammed has changed to Muhammad, and many now write Quran instead of Koran.

24 How is Arabic written?

Arabic is one of several languages written from right to left. That is opposite of how this paragraph is written. Neither direction is inherently forward or backward. It is just what you are used to.

25 Are characters in Arabic different than those used in English?

Yes. English is written in Latin characters. Arabic is written in the 28-character Arabic alphabet. In Arabic, a character may change depending on its placement in the word or sentence. Some Arabic letter combinations are connected like script. Fine writing is called calligraphy and is held in high regard and appreciated as an art form in the Arabic culture. Numbers in Arabic are also different than those in English.

Demographics

26 When did Arab people come to the United States?

Today, most Arab Americans are native-born Americans. The first significant wave of immigration began around 1875. It lasted until about 1920. After a period of restricted immigration, a second wave, sometimes referred to as the brain drain, began in the 1940s. Many people also immigrated to the United States after the 1967 Arab-Israeli war. The 1975-1990 civil war in Lebanon resulted in a large number of Lebanese and Syrian immigrants. The more recent Arab uprisings could bring further immigration, though the U.S. government is becoming more restrictive in granting permanent visas to refugees and others from these countries.

27 Why did Arabs first come to the United States?

Like many peoples who came to the United States, Arabs have come seeking opportunity, security and a better life. Factors in the first wave of immigration were Japanese competition that hurt the Lebanese silk market and a disease in Lebanese vineyards. Most early Arab immigrants were from present-day Lebanon and Syria, and most were Christians.

28 What prompted the second wave of immigration?

After 1940, immigration to the United States was not for economic reasons as much as because of the Arab-Israeli conflict and civil war. This meant that people came from many more places. The second immigration also had many more people who practiced Islam, a religion that was not as familiar in the United States. Immigrants in this group tended to be more financially secure when they arrived, compared to people who had come for economic opportunity. Many people in the second wave were students.

29 What race are Arab Americans?

There are no distinct Arabic physical characteristics. Arabs may have black, brown, blond or red hair and blue, brown or green eyes, and have skin tones that range from very dark to very light. The U.S. Census classifies all people of Arab or Middle Eastern ancestry as white (Caucasian), though many Arab Americans see themselves differently.

30 Are Arabs a minority group?

This depends, in part, on your definition of minority. The U.S. government does not classify Arabs as a minority group for the purposes of employment and housing. Arabs are not defined specifically by race, like some minority groups, but are united by culture and language. Some Arab Americans see minority classification as an impediment to full participation in American life. Others want protection from the same issues affecting people in minority groups, such as stereotyping, exclusion and profiling.

31 Are Arab Americans more closely tied to their country of origin, or to America?

This need not be an either-or issue. Like most first-generation immigrants, Arab Americans have dual loyalties at first, but this changes after a generation or two, by which point most consider themselves Americans. While they may be closely tied to their countries of origin by heritage, most Arab Americans were born in the United States. Even more have U.S. citizenship. This is reflected in the expression, "Truly Arab and fully American."

32 Who are some well-known Arab Americans?

Christa McAuliffe, the teacher/astronaut who died aboard the space shuttle Challenger; Indy 500 winner Bobby Rahal; Mothers Against Drunk Driving founder Candy Lightner; Hollywood actor and producer Tony Shalhoub; Paul Orfalea, the founder of Kinko's; John J. Mack, CEO of Morgan Stanley and DJ Khaled, record producer, radio personality, rapper, DJ and record label executive.

33 Does the U.S. Census Bureau collect data on Arab Americans?

There has been increasing pressure from Arab Americans on the Census Bureau to ask this question. While the census does not specifically classify Arab Americans, it asks an ancestry question on its long form and collects enough data to present some population characteristics. Some of that information is on the U.S. Census Bureau's website at www.census.gov, and is reflected in this guide.

34 What is the educational level of Arab Americans?

The average educational level for Arab Americans is higher than that of non-Arab Americans. More than 89 percent of Arab Americans over 25 have a high school diploma. The proportion of Arab Americans who attend college is higher than the national average. Compared to the norm, Arab Americans are more likely to earn degrees beyond the bachelor's degree, 45 percent to 28 percent. Key factors influencing education are country of origin, length of time in the United States and gender.

35 What occupations do Arab Americans pursue?

Arab Americans work in all occupations. Collectively, they are more likely than others to be self-employed, to be entrepreneurs or to work in sales. About 60 percent of working Arab Americans are executives, professionals, office and sales staff. It varies by area. Arab Americans are most likely to be executives in Washington, D.C., and Anaheim, Calif.; sales people in Cleveland and Anaheim, and manufacturing workers in Detroit. As with all people, employment choices may be influenced by nationality, religion, education, socio-economic status and gender.

36 How do Arab Americans fare economically?

Individually, Arab Americans are at every economic strata of American life. Nationally, Arab-American households have a higher than average median income. Like occupational patterns, this varies by location. Some recent immigrants and refugees are likely to live below the poverty line.

Family

37 What is the role of the family in Arab culture?

The variety of family types among Arab Americans is vast, and influenced by the previously mentioned dimensions of nationality, religion, education, socio-economic status and gender. Generally, family is more important than the individual and more influential than nationality. People draw much of their identity from their role in the family. Historically, this has fostered immigration in which members of an extended family or clan help one another immigrate.

38 Do Arab Americans maintain ties with their home countries?

Many do. They are proud of their home countries and may maintain regular contact with relatives or friends there, just like many other Americans. It is perfectly consistent to have feelings for both their place of origin and their country of citizenship.

39 What are gender roles like for Arab Americans?

These vary tremendously. Some of the variables that affect gender roles are country of origin, whether the family came from a rural or urban area and how long the person's family has been in the United States. Gender roles are also influenced by religion. You'll get very different answers if you ask people individually, and the range you hear about is a more accurate picture of the answer.

40 Are Arab-American households larger than other American households?

Arab-American families are, on average, larger than non-Arab-American families and smaller than families in Arab countries. Traditionally, more children meant more economic contributors for the family. Large families are also a source of pride. The cost of having large families in the United States, however, and adaptation to American customs seem to encourage smaller families. For 2006-2010, the Census Bureau estimated the average size of all U.S. households to be 2.5 and the average for all Arab-American households at 2.93.

41 What kind of relationship does cousin mean to Arab Americans?

The same as for other Americans, though Arabs may differentiate between maternal and paternal cousins when they refer to them.

42 Do generations of Arab Americans live together?

Sometimes, especially with people who have more recently arrived in the United States, but this can be true of non-Arabs as well and is not a distinguishing characteristic of Arab Americans.

43 Do Arab Americans typically get married at a younger age than non-Arabs?

One marriage statistic that stands out is that Arab-American adults are more likely to be married than non-Arab adult Americans. The average age of first marriages is not clear, but it is higher for Arab Americans, most of whom were born in the United States, than for adults in Arab countries. Assimilation and pursuit of college degrees and careers have been cited as factors for this.

44 Are marriages arranged?

This is very rare in the United States, except among some of the most recent immigrants. Remember that most Arab Americans were born here, and that they frequently marry people from other cultures. In the case where a marriage is arranged, a parent may recommend someone from another family or from the country of origin, but the child is not forced to marry that person. More typically, couples meet and ask their families' approval before getting engaged, or make their own decision and then tell their families. As with many cultures, it can be traditional for couples seeking to marry to ask the blessing of all parents.

45 Do Arab Americans prefer to marry each other?

As with many people, in-group marriage may be encouraged to preserve heritage, but Arabs and non-Arabs frequently marry one other. Religious differences among Arab Americans, in fact, may make it more desirable to marry a non-Arab of similar religious background than to marry an Arab of a different religion.

46 Are there Arab conventions for naming children?

Depending on their religion, Arabs often name their children after people in the Bible or the Quran. Both holy books contain many of the same people. For instance, Yusif is Joseph, Mussa is Moses, Ibrahim is Abraham and Issa is Jesus. Muslims often name boys after Muhammad, the prophet who founded Islam. Although names can indicate religion, don't assume this to be always true. Arab tradition may call for the father's name to be the middle name of sons and daughters.

47 What does the title Umm or Abu mean as part of a name?

It is a common way of calling someone using the name of the eldest son. Umm means mother of. Abu means father of. "Umm Adam" is "mother of Adam." This is what friends might call her, as a sign of respect.

48 What does it mean when an Arab refers to someone as Auntie?

This is done in many cultures. It is a sign of respect, not necessarily family relationship. An Arab American might call an older Arab female or male "auntie" ("amty") or "uncle" ("ammo"). They might call grandma "teta" or "siti" and grandpa "jiddo" or "sidi." Many Arab Americans do not use these terms at all. You can show respect by starting with courtesy titles like Mr. and Ms. If people like to be addressed differently, they will tell you how.

Customs, Clothing & Food

49 Why do some Arab women wear garments that cover their head or face?

This practice is a religious practice, related to Islam, and not a specifically Arab tradition. While some say that veiling denigrates women, some women who dress this way say it liberates them. Some say it is more oppressive to be expected to dress in revealing ways. This practice of modesty, called hijab, is not universally observed by Muslim women and varies by region and class. Some governments have, at times, banned veiling and at other times required it. In American families, a mother, a daughter or a sister might decide to cover her head while the other does not. Most Arab Americans dress like other Americans.

50 What does hijab entail?

One interpretation is that everything should be covered except hands, face and feet. Long clothing and a scarf would accomplish this, and the headscarf might be called a hijab or chador. The long, robe-like garment is called an abayah, burqa, jilbab or chador. The face veil is called a niqab. In Iraq and Saudi Arabia especially, a woman may wear a cloak that covers her head. Beneath a robe, a woman might wear a traditional dress, casual clothes or a business suit. The veil, in particular, has been made controversial by governments, gender politics and religious biases. Few Muslim women in the United States wear veils.

51 Some Arab men wear a checked garment on their heads. What is that?

It is called a kafiyyeh and it is traditional, not religious. Wearing the kafiyyeh is similar to an African American wearing traditional African attire, or an Indian woman wearing a sari. The kafiyyeh shows identity and pride in culture. Different styles and colors of the kafiyyeh can have significance.

52 Why do some Arab women dress in black?

Remember that black is a popular color in contemporary fashion and may not have any special significance. When it does, it may be a sign of mourning. Black, when worn in mourning, may be worn for a few days to many years.

53 Why do some Arab men decline to shake hands with women?

This is not true for most Arab men. Some adherents of Islam do decline to shake hands with women, citing religious reasons, but this rarely happens with Arab Americans. Men may help women who are injured or who need assistance.

54 What is an appropriate way to greet an Arab American?

It's easy. It is done the same way other Americans greet each other. Just say, "hi!" Most Arab Americans grew up in the United States and do not require special greetings. Just be yourself, and watch for cues. A smile, a nod and a word of greeting are appropriate in most situations. Some Muslims feel it is inappropriate for unrelated men and women to shake hands. If a hand is extended and the other person touches their palm to his or her chest instead, this is a sign of a respectful greeting and no cause for offense or embarrassment.

55 What are the customs for paying compliments?

Again, be yourself and be observant. In most cases, there is no reason to behave differently from how you would with anyone else. For some recent immigrants, be a little more reserved. Complimenting a possession may be misunderstood and the person, out of generosity and hospitality, may feel compelled to offer you the item. There can be differences between one person and another, even a parent and child, so don't assume a specific courtesy is more authentic than another.

56 What is Middle Eastern food like?

Tasty! It is varied, but has some staples. Wheat is used in bread, pastries, salads and main dishes. Rice is often cooked with vegetables, lamb, chicken or beef. Lamb and mutton are more common than other meats. Fish is popular. Arab recipes use many beans, including fava and lentils, as well as vegetables including eggplant, zucchini, cauliflower, spinach, onions, parsley, okra, tomatoes and chickpeas. Common spices include cumin, nutmeg, cinnamon, sumac, allspice, turmeric, caraway and cardamom. Arabic food can be very vegetarian-friendly. The Mediterranean diet has become fashionable in the United States as a healthy way to eat.

57 Why is the food varied?

There are bound to be different food traditions, since the Middle East is made up of more than 20 countries. Recipes also fuse and recombine when brought into America's diverse regions. Finally, Muslims all over the world follow a diet that is halal, meaning permissible under Islamic law. Pork is not halal. The criteria for other meats include the source and the way in which it was butchered and processed.

58 What is that elaborate pipe people sometimes smoke?

It is a water pipe that filters and cools tobacco smoke. The smoke is usually flavored with apple, honey, strawberry, mint, mango or apricot. Such pipes are smoked in many parts of the world and go by several names, including sheesha, hookah and argilah, or argeelah.

Religion

59 What religion are Arab Americans?

They belong to many religions. Most are Christians.
According to the Arab American Institute, about 63 percent
of Arab Americans are Christians, 24 percent are Muslims
and 13 percent follow other religions, including Judaism, or
have no religious affiliation.

60 Are there further distinctions?

Yes. About 35 percent of Arab Americans are Roman Rite
or Eastern Catholics. Eastern Rite includes Maronite and
Melkite Catholics. About 18 percent of all Arab Americans
are Eastern Orthodox or Oriental Orthodox Christians and
about 10 percent are Protestant. Arab American Muslims
include Shi'a, Sunni or Alawite Muslims. To be sure about a
person's religion, it is OK to ask.

61 What is Eastern rite or Eastern Orthodox?

These are designations for Christian churches that share
some similarities, but that have different histories. Eastern
rite churches are part of the Catholic Church with roots
in the Middle East. They include Maronites, Melkites
and Chaldeans. Eastern Orthodox churches, which are
independent from Vatican authority, include the Syrian and

Coptic churches. In the United States, the largest branch of Eastern Orthodox is the Antiochian.

62 Who are Coptics?

The word Copt is derived from the Greek word for Egyptian, and Coptic was the native language of Egypt before Arabic prevailed. Today, the word refers to Coptic Christians. Although linguistically and culturally classified as Arabs, many Copts consider themselves to be ethnically distinct from other Egyptians. The Copts in Egypt used to number about 10 million, although many are being forced to emigrate.

63 Are most Arabs worldwide Muslim?

Yes, although most Arab Americans are Christians. In Lebanon, the largest ancestral homeland for Arab Americans, almost 20 religions are practiced. There, the population is about 54 percent Muslim and 41 percent Christian. There are more than 20 million Christians in the Arab world.

64 Is Islam mostly an Arab religion?

No. Only about 12 percent of the world's Muslims are Arabs. There are more Muslims in the country of Indonesia, for example, than in all Arab countries combined. Large populations of Muslims also live in India, Iran, other parts of East Asia and sub-Saharan Africa. Islam has a strong Arab flavor because the religion's holiest places are in the Middle East, and the Quran was written in Arabic. Islam is the world's second largest religion after Christianity.

65 What is the Quran?

The Quran is the holy book for Muslims, who believe it contains the word of God revealed to the prophet Muhammad. The Quran has many passages that are similar to those in the Bible and Torah, which Muslims also regard as holy books. Quran is the preferred English spelling. Other spellings are Qur'an and Koran. Variations come from transliterating Arabic into English.

66 What is the difference between Islam and Muslim?

Islam is the religion, and a Muslim is a person who follows the religion. It is like the difference between Christianity and Christian. The adjective is Islamic.

67 What are the five pillars of Islam?

The five pillars are minimum sacred obligations for followers who are able to observe them. They are: belief in the shehada, the statement that "There is no god but God, and Muhammad is his prophet;" salat, or prayer five times a day; zakat, the sharing of alms with the poor; fasting during the holy month of Ramadan, and the hajj, a pilgrimage to Mecca in Saudi Arabia.

68 What is Ramadan?

Ramadan is the ninth month of the Muslim calendar. It is a month of fasting whose end is marked with a celebration called Eid al-Fitr. During this month of self-discipline and purification, Muslims abstain from food, drink and sex from before sunrise until sundown. At night, however, they may feast. The Islamic calendar is based on the cycles of the moon and has 354 days, so Ramadan does not always occur at the same time of year according to the 365-day civil calendar commonly used in the United States.

69 What are important Islamic observances?

One of the most important Islamic holidays is Eid al-Fitr, the "Feast of Breaking the Fast" at the end of the month-long observance of Ramadan. Another is Eid al-Adha, the Feast of the Sacrifice, commemorating God's intervention that prevented Ibrahim's sacrifice of his son. There are other holidays, as well, but do not assume that a holiday or practice observed at one mosque is observed by all.

70 What does hajj mean?

Al hajj refers to the pilgrimage to Mecca by millions of Muslims once each year. It is a milestone event in a Muslim's life. A man who makes the trip is recognized with the title hajj, for example, "Hajj Ahmad." For women, the title is hajjah, though pronunciation varies. Muslims who are financially and physically able to do so are expected to make the journey at least once in their lifetime. Many like to do it more than once. Christians can also perform a hajj to Jerusalem.

71 What is the difference between Sunni and Shi'a Muslims?

Historically, these are the two main branches of Islam. The distinction has to do with the successor of the prophet Muhammad. Sunnis believe his successors were elected religious leaders; Shi'a believe that the prophet appointed his cousin, Ali ibn Abi Taleb. That's the short and simple answer. There are other differences and new ones have arisen over the years. There also are separate groups and movements within each branch. In the United States, Muslim unity often overshadows this division. Most Muslims worldwide and in the United States are Sunnis, though Shi'a dominate in some communities. Most Muslims in Iraq, Bahrain, Lebanon and Iran (a non-Arab country) are Shi'a.

72 Are there conventions for entering a mosque?

There can be and one should look for cues or ask. One generally should take shoes off before entering the prayer room and you might see a mat or shelves to place them on. Look for a sign from your host, or for a place to leave your shoes. Women should dress modestly and may be asked to cover their heads. It is polite to ask in advance. Men should wear long pants and shirts. Men and women generally pray in different areas.

73 Who is an imam?

This is the leader of prayer at a mosque. He might also be called a sheikh. Religious leaders give sermons on Friday, the holiest day of the typical Islamic week, and provide spiritual guidance. An imam or sheikh might also be the administrator.

74 Where is the headquarters for Islam?

Islam does not have the same kind of hierarchy as some other religions. There is no top official for Islam. Muslim mosques, or masjids, and associations are independent. Muslims are not required to be members of a mosque.

75 What is the Nation of Islam?

This African American religious group evolved in the 20th century with some different practices from those followed by most Muslims. Most African-American Muslims in the United States are not part of the Nation of Islam and many Muslims see it as something entirely different from their faith.

76 What does Allah mean?

Allah means God. Arabic-speaking Christians, Muslims and Jews use the same word when they talk about God. When translating Arabic expressions, translate all the words for consistency. The translation of "Allahu akbar," for example, would be "God is great" or "God is greater," not "Allah is great."

77 Why do Muslims face east when they pray?

Muslims pray facing the Kaaba, the Holy House, at Mecca, the holiest city in Islam. Muslims in other countries face different directions, depending on where they are in relation to Mecca. And, yes, there's an app for that.

Politics

78 Are Arab Americans active in U.S. politics?

Yes and more so with the passage of time. Arab Americans vote, run for office and get elected. Arab American organizations are working to get them involved in American politics and to be counted. Arab Americans are not a large number of voters nationally and do not vote in one bloc. The 2000 campaign was the first in which both major presidential candidates addressed Arab Americans.

79 How do Arabs vote?

A poll released by the Arab American Institute shortly before the 2012 presidential election showed growing disassociation from both major political parties. Fifty-two percent preferred Democrat Barack Obama and 28 percent preferred Republican Mitt Romney. That represented a large decline from Obama's 2008 support among Arab Americans. The institute also asked about party affiliation. Forty-six percent said they were Democrats and 22 percent said they were Republicans, an all-time low. Twenty-four percent identified themselves as independent.

80 Do Arab Americans run for office?

They do. In 2012, for example, more than 20 ran for state and federal offices. Winners included four Republican U.S. representatives: Nick Rahall, Va.; Richard Hanna, New York; Justin Amash, Mich., and Darrell Issa, R-California.

81 Who are other prominent Arab-American politicians?

They have included U.S. Senate Majority Leader George J. Mitchell, D-Maine; former Energy Secretary Spencer Abraham; former secretary of Health and Human Services Donna Shalala; former New Hampshire governor and White House chief of staff John Sununu, and 2000 presidential candidate and consumer advocate Ralph Nader. Four governors have been of Arab descent. Three were Republicans and one was a Democrat.

82 Is there an Arab lobby?

There is not an Arab lobby in the sense of a monolithic, controlling body. There are several organizations that lobby in behalf of a variety of issues, including domestic and international concerns. One is the Arab American Institute, which supports presidential and congressional candidates receptive to Arab-American concerns. Others are the American Arab Anti-Discrimination Committee, a civil rights group, the National Network for Arab American Communities and the Arab American Political Action Committee in Michigan.

Terminology

83 When do I say Arab, Arabic or Arabian?

Arab is a noun for a person, and it can be used as an adjective, as in "Arab country." Arabic is the name of the language and generally is not used as an adjective. Arabian is an adjective that refers to Saudi Arabia, the Arabian Peninsula, or for things, such as an Arabian horse. When ethnicity or nationality is relevant, it is more precise and accurate to specify the country by using Lebanese, Yemeni or whatever is appropriate.

84 Do people prefer Arab American, or American Arab?

Arab American is preferred, like Irish American or German American.

85 How should I refer to a single Arab American person?

If you can be specific, say the country that person is descended from. For example: "of Lebanese heritage," or "of Jordanian descent." Arab Americans come from many places and religions and have different perspectives, so even individuals of the same nationality have different opinions.

People of different nationalities might have very different views. Many Arab Americans have only ever lived in the United States. Knowing the country of origin for someone's family is only a beginning.

86 What does Mohammedanism mean?

That is outdated and inaccurate. Instead, use Islam for the religion, Muslim for a follower of the religion and derivatives of these words.

87 Is it Muslim or Moslem?

It is Muslim.

88 Who is a sheikh?

A sheikh can be the leader of a family, a village, a tribe or a mosque. Press accounts popularized the term "oil-rich sheikh." This contributed to the misconception that the people who became wealthy from oil were sheikhs, and that sheikhs had oil money. Neither is true.

Stereotype & Superstition

89 How do movies and TV shows portray Arab characters?

In "Guilty: Hollywood's Verdict on Arabs after 9/11," communications scholar Jack Shaheen wrote, "More than a century of reel injurious Arab stereotypes, including the majority of post-9/11 movies, have helped us 'kill people with our minds.' Instead of mainstream studios projecting Arabs as regular folks—family men, women, and children—films continued defaming them as the unkempt, unscrupulous enemy 'other.'" Later in the book he wrote, "I believe thoughtful imagemakers are beginning to rollback slanderous portraits and create fuller, more complicated Arab characters and stories."

90 Are Arabs oil-rich?

Some are, most aren't. The area around the Persian Gulf is one of several oil-producing areas in the world, but not all Arab countries produce oil, and very few Arabs are rich from oil.

91 Are Arabs mostly a nomadic desert people?

No. Most live in urban areas, just as most Americans do. Portrayals of Arabs as desert dwellers have distorted the picture. Bedouins, nomadic people depicted in movies, make up only about 2 percent of Arab people. Cairo, the largest city in the Arab world, has about 9 million people, a little more than New York City, the largest city in America. Arab countries have a range of climates. Many have coastal areas and some have mountainous areas that get snow. Arab people come from latitudes from as far south as just below the equator to as far north as approximately Lexington, Ky.

92 Are Arabs terrorists?

Terrorists of many ethnicities operate all around the globe. High-profile attacks have brought U.S. attention to terrorists from the Middle East, and the U.S. State Department has identified many groups with Arab connections. However, it is inaccurate to assume that, because people are Arabs or Arab Americans, they are involved in terrorism or, when an attack occurs, that Arabs must be involved.

93 What is meant by the phrase "Islamic fundamentalist"?

This is complex. The term fundamentalist, whether applied to Muslims or Christians, is a largely Western construct that implies political and religious conservatism and, sometimes, extremism. Some groups make no distinction between their cause and their interpretation of the religion. The term "Islamic fundamentalist" has been used to refer to people who cite Islam to justify political actions. Fairness and accuracy mean attributing political actions to the group, government or party responsible, and not just to the religion, which may have millions of followers with different beliefs. The same is true of using "Islamist" as a shorthand adjective for "threats" or "militants." It is too broad.

94 Is Islam a violent religion?

The Quran teaches nonviolence. Individual verses should not be quoted to convey the meaning of the whole book, but in the wake of modern terror attacks, theological scholars have backed that up. Throughout history, political groups and leaders have used many religions to justify nationalistic or territorial violence. Shaheen wrote, "We should remember that the 'people of the book'—Jews, Christians, and Muslims—are all children of Abraham. All three religions emphasize an ethic of humane behavior and belief in one God who reveals his will through the sacred scriptures. Central to the three faiths is peace, which is reflected in the similarities of their greetings. Shalom aliechem in Hebrew, pax vobiscum in Latin, salaam alaikum in Arabic: 'Peace be with you.'"

95 Are Arab-American women subservient to men?

No sweeping statement reflects all the roles of Arab women. They range from leaders of matriarchal societies to independent businesswomen to women living under extreme repression. Gender roles can be the product of acculturation and assimilation and might have to do with country of origin, family, religious interpretation and personality.

96 Are women who wear scarves and other coverings oppressed?

Ask some of them. They will probably tell you that they dress this way out of choice. It is not unusual to find that women from the same family follow different practices. Some say that they feel the oppressed women are the ones who feel pressure to dress in revealing ways.

97 What is that charm with the eye or an eye on a hand?

Often worn as jewelry, the hamsa was a non-religious symbol for good luck or protection that pre-dated Islam. It is seen in many cultures, including Latin American, Greek, Ethiopian and Turkish. People from many traditions and religions have adopted it. Some Muslims call it the "hand of Fatima." She was a daughter of the prophet Muhammad.

98 How can I meet Arab Americans in my community?

In cities where there are large populations, this is easy. You can find restaurants, stores, markets and other businesses with Arabic names or writing on them. Look for organizations, community centers, churches and mosques that might be Arab-related. Use these as beginning points to meet more people, and not just recent immigrants. To find Arab Americans in places where they are less prevalent, try some of the organizations in the resources section of this guide.

99 Are there big misconceptions about Arab Americans that I should avoid?

Here are three:

- Arab Americans are part of a cultural group, connected by language and tradition. There is not an Arab religion.

- Arab Americans are distinct from other groups they are sometimes clustered with such as Indians, Iranians or Chaldeans.

- Like the rest of Americans, most Arab Americans oppose terrorism and have extra reasons for that. They know that acts of terrorism can be directed against them, as Americans, and attributed to them because of their heritage.

100 How can I learn more?

We're glad you asked. This guide is just an introduction. Any one of the 100 questions in it has answers that would fill a book. We have listed some resources for further study in the following pages. We also encourage you to get out and talk to people.

Books and Publications

Abraham, Nabeel, Sally Howell, Andrew Shryock and Hayan Charara. *Arab Detroit 9/11: Life in the Terror Decade*. Detroit: Wayne State University Press, 2011.

Baker, Wayne, Sally Howell, Amaney Jamal and Ann Chih Lin. *Citizenship and Crisis: Arab Detroit After 9/11*. New York: Russell Sage Foundation, 2009.

Barakat, Halim. *The Arab World: Society, Culture and State*. Berkeley and Los Angeles: University of California Press, 1993.

Bayoumi, Moustafa. *How Does It Feel to Be a Problem?* New York: Penguin Books, 2009.

Freedman, Robert O., ed. *The Middle East and the Peace Process: The Impact of the Oslo Accords*. Gainesville: University Press of Florida, 1998.

Freidman, Thomas L. *From Beirut to Jerusalem*. New York: Doubleday, 1989.

Haiek, John R., ed. *The Arab American Almanac*. 6th ed. Glendale: News Circle Publishing House, 2010.

Hooglund, Eric J., ed. *Crossing the Waters: Arabic-Speaking Immigrants to the United States Before 1940*. Washington, D.C.: Smithsonian Institution Press, 1987.

Malek, Alia, ed. *A Country Called Amreeka*. New York: Free Press, 2009.

---. *Patriot Acts Narratives of Post-9/11 Injustice (Voice of Witness)*. San Francisco: McSweeney's and Voice of Witness, 2011.

Mattawa, Khale and Munir Akash. *Post Gibran: Anthology of New Arab American Writing*. West Bethesda: Kitab Inc., dist. by Syracuse University Press, 1999.

Samia, El-Badry. *The Arab-American Market*. American Demographics, January 1994.

Shaheen, Jack. *Arab and Muslim Stereotyping in American Popular Culture*. Washington, D.C.: Georgetown University Center for Muslim-Christian Understanding, 1997.

---. *Guilty: Hollywood's Verdict on Arabs After 9/11*. Northampton: Olive Branch Press, 2008.

---. *Reel Bad Arabs: How Hollywood Vilifies a People*. 2nd ed. Northampton: Olive Branch Press, 2009.

---. *The TV Arab*. Bowling Green: Bowling Green State University Press, 1984.

Shipler, David. *Arab and Jew: Wounded Spirits in a Promised Land*. New York: Penguin, 1987.

Suleiman, Michael W. *Arabs in America: Building a New Future*. Philadelphia: Temple University Press, 1999.

International Press Institute. *Use With Care: A Reporter's Glossary of Loaded Language in the Israeli-Palestinian Conflict*, 2013.

Zogby, James, ed. *Taking Root, Bearing Fruit: the Arab-American Experience*. Washington, D.C.: American-Arab Anti-Discrimination Committee, 1984.

---. *Arab Voices: What They Are Saying to Us, and Why it Matters*. New York: Palgrave Macmillan, 2012.

Organizations

- American Arab Anti-Discrimination Committee, www.adc.org
- ACCESS, www.accesscommunity.org
- Arab American and Chaldean Council, myacc.org
- Arab American Institute, www.aaiusa.org
- Arab American National Museum, www.arabamericanmuseum.org
- Arab American Political Action Committee, aapac.org
- Council on American-Islamic Relations, www.cair.com
- Lebanese American Heritage Club, lahc.org
- National Arab American Bar Association, www.naaba.org
- National Arab American Medical Association, www.naama.com
- National Network for Arab American Communities, www.nnaac.org

If you enjoyed this book, you may also enjoy

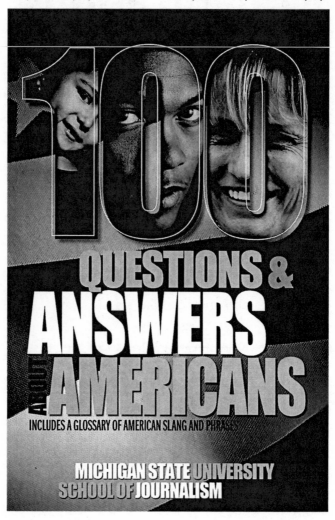

This questions and answers guide from the Michigan
State University School of Journalism provides 100
answers to basic questions about Americans.

http://news.jrn.msu.edu/culturalcompetence/

ISBN: 978-1-939880-20-8

If you enjoyed this book, you may also enjoy

100 QUESTIONS & ANSWERS ABOUT EAST ASIAN CULTURES

MICHIGAN STATE UNIVERSITY SCHOOL OF JOURNALISM

This questions and answers guide from the Michigan State University School of Journalism provides 100 answers to basic questions about East Asian cultures.

http://news.jrn.msu.edu/culturalcompetence/

ISBN: 978-939880-50-5

If you enjoyed this book, you may also enjoy

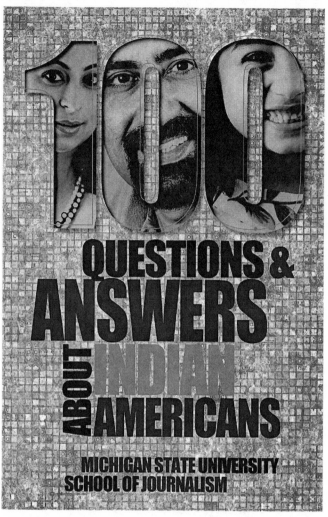

This questions and answers guide from the Michigan
State University School of Journalism provides 100
answers to basic questions about Indian Americans.

http://news.jrn.msu.edu/culturalcompetence/

ISBN: 978-1-939880-00-0

If you enjoyed this book, you may also enjoy

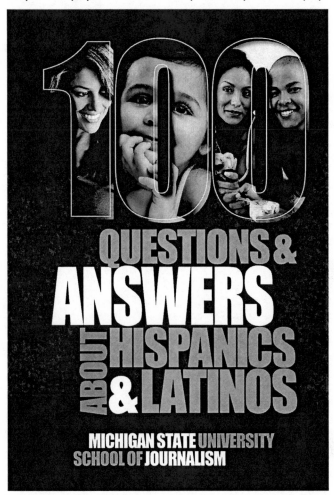

This questions and answers guide from the Michigan
State University School of Journalism provides 100
answers to basic questions about Hispanics and Latinos.

http://news.jrn.msu.edu/culturalcompetence/

ISBN: 978-1-939880-44-4

CPSIA information can be obtained
at www.ICGtesting.com
Printed in the USA
FFOW03n2311030416
22868FF